Lumumba Speaks

Quotes That Drive The Liberation Movement

The Voice of Patrick Lumumba

Lumumba Speaks ~~~ *Patrick Lumumba*

Copyright © 2020 Patrick Alexander

Book Cover Design by Ellen "Butterflyy" Allen

Published by PLP --- Patricia Lee Publishing

ISBN 978-1-7353946-1-9

ATTENTION CORPORATIONS, UNIVERSITIES, COLLEGES AND PROFESSIONAL ORGANIZATIONS: Quantity discounts are available on bulk purchases of this book for educational, gift purposes, or as premiums for increasing magazine subscriptions or renewals. Special books or book excerpts can also be created to fit specific needs. For information, please contact Patricia Lee Publishing, 4511 Bluebell St; Memphis, TN 38109, 901-255-4848 or mytrusense@gmail.com also view mytrusensememphis.com

Lumumba Speaks ~~~ Patrick Lumumba

He speaks with the voice of the lion and sees with the eyes of the eagle and the tiger, uses the wisdom of the owl, the sense of the ants, the force of the red kangaroo, the strength of the bear, the mind of the fox, the inner strength such as that of the rhinoceros, the inner height likened unto that of the elephant, hands likened to that of the octopus with the inner soul of a HueMan and moves with the whistling of the Wind. **My Tru-Sense** likens him to the whirlwind that the Honorable Marcus Mosiah Garvey told us to look for as he is the embodiment of Patrice Lumumba, Malcolm X, Kwame Ture, the Honorable Elijah Muhammad, John Henrik Clark and many of the Greats of our Ankhcestars---we are delighted to introduce to you quotes from the one and only Patrick Alexander known to us in our time as Patrick Lumumba---The Khing of the Black Liberation Movement – **The Black Panther ---OUR totem of STRENGTH AND POWER**

He is the facilitator and founder of the Black Liberation Movement in Coldwater, Mississippi---2015

Lumumba Speaks ~~~ Patrick Lumumba

From the desk of Patrick Lumumba, Chief Organizing Facilitator, of the Mississippi based Black Liberation Movement:

To my beloved and dear Black family, my sleep has been disturbed this morning in the same fashion it was disturbed approximately 5 years ago by the spirit and inspiration of those who came before us (our Ancestors) invoking me to pronounce the Black Liberation Movement. This morning my message to you flows from that same inspiration.

Black People, know that we are the most resilient, most durable, most humanitarian, most reliant, most scrutinized, most attacked, most used, most scapegoated, most discriminated, most scorned, most ostracized, most _____ (you can just fill in the blank)............................ BUT, WE STILL HERE!

Even amidst the concoction of COVID19 and the media's narratives that twist and gerrymander the target on our collective black backs, we persevere and still navigate in our discombobulated drunken stupor still reeling from all the other blows historically dealt to us by an unforgiving and merciless world hellbent on destroying black people.......................BUT, WE STILL HERE!

Everybody the world over is having to figure out how to deal with COVID19, but WE (black people), been dealing with COVID19 like state of emergency level stresses for centuries now that are unrivaled in the documents of human records. Nobody else deals with the social injustices, the inhumane treatment, the forced destitution, the isolated discrimination, and mass exploitation, as WE (black people) have..........................BUT, WE STILL HERE!

So, by the sheer nature of our circumstances, there should be a natural emergence of CHANGE brewing in our midst.

If out of oppression CHANGE comes, then where should we be looking for that CHANGE to come from? It is "clear" to me that it is only one word that defines this change, that word is LIBERATION. Point Blank! If you find yourself amongst black people who are not talking liberated talk then you should be finding yourself another crowd to consume your time with because your time there is essentially pointless as it pertains to real progress. LIBERATION should be on the tips of ALL black peoples tongues, even our babies, the first word their little pallets should form to utter is LIBERATION. Our circumstances demand it! It is mandated by nature! And it is eminent!

Pronouncing the Black Liberation Movement 5 years ago was nothing more than our historic collective struggle re-emerging as an "Organized Response"......(I hope y'all caught that). The Black Liberation Movement is the manifestation of our MORAL CONVICTION, CONSCIOUSNESS, CHARACTER, and COURAGE! The Black Liberation Movement is our Ancestors speaking through us with a resounding voice that demands RESPECT!

That's why I lead with extreme confidence, boldness, fearlessness, vigor, pride, self-worth, character, and DETERMINATION!
Now, I leave you with one question.......WILL YOU HELP?
Peace Blessings and Power,Lumumba

Lumumba Speaks ~~~ Patrick Lumumba

We must be wise like the Ancestors
We must plan like the Scholars
We must have determination like the Lion
We Will Win ~ Lumumba

Love Your Enemy...Turned the other cheek...Love those who despitefully use you...

Now just how well has that worked out in the grand scheme of things for the melinated P.O.W.s (Black/Afrikan/Indigenous) in this land we call America? □
Lemme tell y'all something and be real clear about it: No RELIGION comes before the survival of my RACE! .... Obviously the religious package that has been shoved down our collective throats and digested hook, line, and sinker is diametrically opposing to the survival of BLACK people and conducive to the long suffering of BLACK people. I'M NOT AFRAID TO TELL Y'ALL WHAT MANY OF YOUR PASTORS "KNOW".... but they feel just like the white man feel ... [If it ain't broke don't fix it] □▩♂□
We gonna have to take on the responsibility and have courage enough to devise something that works spiritually and PRACTICALLY for "US"........I'm ready

to sit at that table ~ Lumumba

The societal standard bar for the BLACK man to be worth anything in the eyes of MOST black women is getting higher and higher...when all it takes for her to be a Goddess (by her own definition) is to posses the ability to give birth....☐ So if you're a Goddess that gives birth to a black MALE child 👶■ then by birthright what is he? ☐ The gender war that we find ourselves immersed in has taken precedence over the REAL WAR we both have been faced with since white supremacy decided it would devalue the quality of black life unforgivingly. It's up to us to recognize this and withdraw our swords ☐ from each other's throats and begin to focus on COMMUNITY UNITY & BLACK LOVE 1st. ☝ ■#BlackLiberationMovement

Lumumba Speaks   ~~~ Patrick Lumumba

Our Ancient Afrikan Ancestors were very wise...I'm gonna call them the Triple A's(Ancient Afrikan Ancestors)...rightfully so because an "A" is the grade they get from me for just being fundamentally wise.
Here's my logic:
The Triple A's: Worshipped the SUN because they understood simply that it
gives life. ☐■♂☐
While we today, I'm gonna refer to this modern day Negro as the Triple S's (Super Smart Sambos)
The Triple S's: Worship the White MAN that simply takes life. ☐■♂☐
I know this is a very "rudimentary" post to you so-called highly evolved Triple S's...but it's a necessary mirror to look at and lens to look through.........peace.

Lumumba Speaks   ~~~   Patrick Lumumba

When I speak I'm not just ranting to kill time...everything spoken from this platform has Aim & Purpose.... I've learned from some of our greatest teachers and I'm still learning...my knowledge is NOT unfounded, void of substance, or reckless. Trust that. I just scare most of you because my effort is to make these teacher's beautiful messages APPLICABLE.....I'm a student/Warrior....I have the discipline to learn and the courage to act on what I've learned.....and that's where the roads separate for most of us.
We won't perish for the lack of Knowledge, will perish if we don't establish the Courage to APPLY.
#BlackLiberationMovement

Facebook posts are not gonna change our conditions BUT they can surely provoke the thoughts and mindsets that can ~ Lumumba #BlackLiberationMovement

Up this Grand Day to pay homage, honor, and RESPECT to the ancestors Alfred "Skip" Robinson the later known Aziz Muhammad.... Great fighter in North Mississippi and abroad on behalf of Black People 🙊■♂️□..... STUDY HIM! A lot of y'all parents know him and probably afraid to this day to utter his name! Don't play with it! #BlackLiberationMovement

When I meet black people who don't see the relevance and the purpose of Black Liberation, I always leave wondering actually how tight are the grips of White Supremacy around their necks? Is it:
•Job Secuity
•Inherit Fear
•Friendship Maintenance
•Ourstorical Ignorance
•Arrogance
•Stockholm Syndrome (love for oppressor)
*Religion(maybe should be at top of list) ☐
•All Of The Above
#BlackLiberationMovement

Lumumba Speaks ~~~ Patrick Lumumba

We turning everything into a gender War(Black woman v/s Black man) and forgetting the real War and white folk laughing ~ Lumumba

Lumumba Speaks ~~~ Patrick Lumumba

Education in America is more a socialization process than a true educational experience...Black people obtain job security in the white corporate sectors NOT because you're so brilliantly educated BUT because you meet the social non-threatening subservient requirements necessary to perform a task and to fit in as a black person who seeks white adulation and an income ~ Lumumba

Lumumba Speaks   ~~~ Patrick Lumumba

Whom so ever is the Greatest among you let him be you SERVANT not your LEADER...the greatest amongst us see our conditions, hear our conditions, breathe our conditions, live our conditions, and the GREATEST amongst us will DIE in dedication to changing our conditions ~ Lumumba
#BlackLiberationMovement

Lumumba Speaks ~~~ Patrick Lumumba

No individual black man/woman is above the condition of his/her people...PERIOD!

Our lack of organization renders us extremely vulnerable and easily domesticated in the throes of our fight against this system... we MUST organize. We pseudo-enjoy a quasi freedom.....when in reality MASSA just pushed the fence line back ~ Lumumba
#LetsGetFree
#BlackLiberationMovement

Lumumba Speaks   ~~~ Patrick Lumumba

Environment shapes heredity but POWER shapes environments, we must focus on building POWER ~ Lumumba

Lumumba Speaks ~~~ Patrick Lumumba

The Black Panther of The Delta...Lumumba...The Facilitator... by whatever name you call me just know it all stands for BLACK POWER ☐▮
#BlackLiberationMovement

Lumumba Speaks ~~~ Patrick Lumumba

This is a picture I took Friday in GREENWOOD, Ms on my way to GREENVILLE, Ms of the biggest cotton gin in the world which is only right because GREENWOOD, Ms is the cotton capital of the WOLRD! The other two pics below are the pictures I took the next day (Saturday) in TUNICA, Ms which also compose the MISSISSIPPI DELTA the land that makes all this "Wealth Building" possible...............do y'all see where I'm going with this? ☐ #LandIsTheBases4Wealth #Do4SelfWhatYouHaveDoneForOthers #LetsBuildOurOwn #BlackLiberationMovement

Lumumba Speaks   ~~~   Patrick Lumumba

Question for Respectful Conversation:
Why can't we (black people) financially commit to SPECIFICALLY BLACK organizations, plans, and agendas?

I swear people just don't understand.

BLACK MOVIE HYSTERIA
Black Panther + Harriet Tubman =
•Black Compromise (It ain't so bad mentality)
•White Heroes/Black Villains
•Lot of Black Dollars spent
•Happy Negroes
•Black folk back to sleep 😒 💤

Lumumba Speaks ~~~ Patrick Lumumba

The Mississippi Delta: I was in awe yesterday as I was riding 61 hwy at this scenery. So I pulled over to soak it all in and snap this picture. Most of you just see a beautiful scene....But I SEE and HEAR much more than that. I SEE the rich fertile land that built astronomical wealth in this country on the backs of our grandparents...and I HEAR the voice of our Ancestors saying "Do for yourselves willingly what you were forced to do for others"...... Peace #BlackLiberationMovement

We crazy bout these backward culture, stupid ass HELL•A•DAYS... running 🏃‍♀️🏃‍♂️ our ass to these folks stores spending money hand over fist to dress our children up like ghosts, vampires, goblins, goons, and whatever other degenerative expression white folk can think of for your children. BUT.... I ask you to buy a BOOK 📖 to help build a CULTURE LIBRARY for your children to learn not of ghosts, goblins, and shit, but of the greatness of themselves YOU TURN YOUR COLLECTIVE HEADS and look the other way! After all, it's all about the Halloween social media PHOTO OPP right?
This is absolutely irresponsible and inappropriate behavior.

Lumumba Speaks ~~~ Patrick Lumumba

I woke up to this!!!! Are u kidding me!☐▇♂☐ Now they have a show "The Preachers" to propagandize and popularize Hollywood style us forgiving those who despitefully use us.......we glorify, pride ourselves, and practice on forgiving white folk.

PSA: Our Cultural Center is fast becoming a nationally recognized and renowned place of cultural history and "Ourstorical" facts. We're presently building a curriculum so that we will be able to teach on an institutional level from ages as young as 3 years old - adult. Now, in order to do this we need to build an extensive library and we need YOUR help family! Today we're launching our BUY A BLACK BOOK DRIVE for the only truly black historical cultural center in North Mississippi. The average cost of a book is $10-$15. Will the black family stand up and assist by Buying a book or two (donate)?.....cash app to $blmms
#TakingControlOfOurFuture #HoldingOurselvesAccountable
#OasisLiteracyProject #RestorationCulturalCenter
#BlackLiberationMovement

Lumumba Speaks ~~~ Patrick Lumumba

When y'all wake up answer this question....... Question: Why "white" men masculinity not considered toxic?

Queens check it out....a proper analysis of OURstory will not suggest that the black man will NOT protect you....a proper assessment will reveal that we're in this war TOGETHER...now stop buying into false narrative last I checked we were BOTH under attack!

I don't post "SAFE" post....... the reason we in the conditions we in now is playing it SAFE... Harriet, Nat, Malcolm, Martin, etc. didn't play it SAFE.

If I had I magic eraser that could erase historical scriptures outta BLACK FOLK bibles, hearts, and minds, I wouldn't waste one second doing it.... the reason is: We get stuck on stupid when it comes to REALITY in comparison to traditional religious dogma. Scripture Example: "My people perish for the lack of Knowledge"............ really?

Reality: At a certain point in time this scripture was truly indicative of our conditions...BUT today I would challenge it with confidence and prove that for the most part we not suffering or perishing for a lack of knowledge as much we are from a lack of COURAGE to apply knowledge...peace.

If you're looking at this picture and your first thoughts are that the place is empty...then your eyes have deceived you because the spirit of our ANCESTORS always fill and occupy this space. Join us sometimes and see for yourself ~Lumumba (The Black Panther of the Delta)
#RNDCC
#BlackLiberationMovement

In case y'all been sleeping thru this decade and haven't noticed BLACK MALE MASCULINITY is under an extreme and very intentional attack. It's not enough that system of white supremacy has imposed a steady assault on black male masculinity since deciding to domesticate us to their mercy as a permanent underclass race of people BUT now our "own" black women have went on record citing strong black male character as TOXIC MASCULINITY while at the same time expressing the lack of protection from the black male! MAKE YO MIND UP...do y'all want coward down emasculated SISSIES who "can't" protect shit that's nothing more than a degenerative product of the system OR do you want a black MAN that's still have 2 balls intact between his legs as your PARTNER to help you fight in this war that we've found our selves in?
#WeNeedToTalk
#BlackLiberationMovement

Y'all using the wrong filters! Stop LIGHTENING yourself up in hopes of being more accommodating, appealing, and so-called attractive.....not being comfortable in yo own skin is a pervasive and growing problem with our people. Learn to be confident being who and what you are NATURALLY ▪️

Lumumba Speaks ~~~ Patrick Lumumba

Grand Day Family:
If you're not part of a black organization that's pushing and building for black people because you fear being attached and pronounced with such.....then all we ask is that you hit that CASH APP.... do like grandma said and feed us with a long handled spoon ☐........
$blmms
#BlackLiberationMovement

If we're afraid and unwilling to TEACH then we certainly can't INSPIRE our people to ACTION ~ Lumumba #BeCourageous #AinNevaScared #BlackLiberationMovement

Lumumba Speaks   ~~~   Patrick Lumumba

True Self Determination...where is it being taught organizationally and institutionally amongst our people?

We use EVERY tool at our disposal to teach. #BlackLiberationMovement

Lumumba Speaks ~~~ Patrick Lumumba

So because I am who I am and because I live On my truth and I understand the division on your mind, the lack of diversity in it, I have chosen to proceed by introducing you to some strong beautiful humans in my life!!! So maybe if I can clean the filtered lenses you view them through , I can provoke change. Cause I will never give up my fight!!!!

This is Patrick Alexander! He is a farmer, a father and a daddy, a business owner and entrepreneur, an activist a zealot, a son, a friend, a sibling, an uncle. How I see him: He is strong and steadfast in his beliefs! He loves his children and his fight is for them! He is brilliant in his stance and his objective! How he exhibits his beliefs is honorable and steadfast. He is kind when he speaks yet bold to his core! He is encouraging and brave and he exudes courage every moment of everyday! I believe in him immensely! It is an honor and a privilege to call him my friend!!!! I SEE him! Now just maybe you can too! #untilyourbecomesour #untilthembecomesus

By Kimberly Michael Schneider

Rising Thoughts:
As I look back over my life a don't see many times where my life has not been a struggle.... Even my birth into the world was a struggle..... I ask for no pity, just letting the pressure off... There is no progress without struggle....but I get tired.

#BlackLiberationMovement

In case y'all been sleeping thru this decade and haven't noticed BLACK MALE MASCULINITY is under an extreme and very intentional attack. It's not enough that system of white supremacy has imposed a steady assault on black male masculinity since deciding to domesticate us to their mercy as a permanent underclass race of people BUT now our "own" black women have went on record citing strong black male character as TOXIC MASCULINITY while at the same time expressing the lack of protection from the black male! MAKE YO MIND UP...do y'all want coward down emasculated SISSIES who "can't" protect shit that's nothing more than a degenerative product of the system OR do you want a black MAN that's still have 2 balls intact between his legs as your PARTNER to help you fight in this war that we've found our selves in?
#WeNeedToTalk
#BlackLiberationMovement

The Moral Character of black men and women MUST be reestablished...we have to reassess our value of SELF and determine that WE are worth fighting for ~ Lumumba

Lumumba Speaks ~~~ Patrick Lumumba

White Supremacy is diametrically opposed and weaponized against the peace of black people...so what we gonna "DO" about that? ~ Lumumba

Lumumba Speaks ~~~ Patrick Lumumba

What's more important to you...your FREEDOM or your LIFE?
~ Lumumba

Lumumba Speaks   ~~~ Patrick Lumumba

I'm pinned to the cross daily...sacrificing my life's energy, creative thought, monetary gains, etc. in dedicated servitude to the people I love.
I know it goes unappreciated...but I've come to the point where it don't even matter if it's appreciated or not...the reciprocal value of knowing I'm doing what's RIGHT and what's NEEDED is enough for me ~ P.A.Theory

We need LOVE POWER ~ Lumumba

Lumumba Speaks ~~~ Patrick Lumumba

BLM: BLACK LIVES MATTER...celebrities, white liberals, LGBTQ 🏳️‍🌈, and black brothers and sisters who need white acceptance to validate their lives, parading around begging white folk to stop the senseless killing of black people.

BLM: BLACK LIBERATION MOVEMENT... Serious no nonsense Black Folk taking our lives and destiny into our own hands UNAPOLOGETICALLY giving ourselves the permission undeterred to determine our own OUTCOME.

#ShitSerious #StopPlaying #KeepActingLikeYouDontSeeThis 👀

Lumumba Speaks   ~~~ Patrick Lumumba

The functionality of Racism/White Supremacy is not destroyed by us thinking we gonna infiltrate a ready made system and change it...the functionality is destroyed by us building a system controlled by US ~ Lumumba

Getting the harvest ready for market tomorrow...order your Black2Health boxes as well...pickup tomorrow in Coldwater on the Square ~ Lumumba

#BlackLiberationMovement

Black Folk: Being afraid to let go of the white man's concept of God is a major impediment to developing the

courage necessary to becoming SELF-DETERMINED...we gave the world "God-Consciousness"...now we acting like little choir boys and girls in the white man's idea of God, which is nothing more than HIMSELF... Let us stop being diffident, sheepish, and Cowardly. Let's establish GOD again ~ Lumumba

Lumumba Speaks ~~~ Patrick Lumumba

COVID19 and all it consists of in my assessment is the biggest white supremacist social engineering POWER WAR for the control of the masses we've seen...my ONLY concern is WHAT BLACK PEOPLE GONE DO ~ Lumumba

At some point y'all gonna have to weaponize yo Christianity against Racism/White Supremacy and join this LIBERATION FIGHT...y'all tryna practice the love of Jesus with white folk while they practice white supremacy on you! 🤔

Lumumba Speaks ~~~ Patrick Lumumba

After all the protest in the wake of the STATE SANCTIONED MURDER of George Floyd...two days ago the Senate still voted "NO" to police 👮 reform...Just thought y'all should know ~ Lumumba

Lumumba Speaks   ~~~ Patrick Lumumba

Are there any BLACK ammunition manufacturers?

Lumumba Speaks ~~~ Patrick Lumumba

One day we will get tired of being tumbled around in the utter chaos of this society...we Will synchronize our unity and build our Nation ~ Lumumba

Shout out to the Black Community of Milwaukee for taking the matters of two missing black girls into their own hands where the local police failed them. Returned the girls to there homes 🏠and burned 🔥downed the sex trafficking house they were being held in.

Special shout out to

Darryl King Rick Farmer II

of the Milwaukee based Black Panther Party for the major role they play, responsibility they assume, and PRIDE they take in the Black community ✊❤~ Lumumba

Don't allow your "PROFESSIONALISM" to stop you from hearing the message of the Black Liberation Movement. DONT sellout Black collective gain for the individual cultural accommodation of white corporate America ~ Lumumba

Lumumba Speaks ~~~ *Patrick Lumumba*

The STOVE is the most underused appliance in the Black home today…we losing our culture Sistahs and Brothas…let's "TIBMIB" (Take It Back & Make It Black ~ Lumumba

Lumumba Speaks ~~~ ***Patrick Lumumba***

The deer 🦌 are straight SAVAGES on our crops 😡😭... I respect nature but this one Black Farmer 👨🏿‍🌾 that's bout to go to WAR with Rudolph's ass!!!! 🧨 ~ Lumumba

Lumumba Speaks   ~~~   Patrick Lumumba

When the Black Man becomes inherently aware and able to articulate his own systematic oppression and willingness to do something about it he becomes a THREAT...public enemy #1 ~ Lumumba

The Black Liberation Movement is a grassroots POWER BUILDING ORGANIZATION...most of us have only built POWER for the traditional oppressors of our people in return for a paycheck...we're looking for the Black Experts who're ready to focus their skill set on building Power "specifically" for us ~ Lumumba

Lumumba Speaks   ~~~ Patrick Lumumba

Remove the BULL SHITTERS from your midst if you plan on getting anything of value done ~ Lumumba

Come to Coldwater, Mississippi on the Square and see Sistah

Crystal Denise

marketing the produce and products of the Movement...we have an array: Cabbage 🥦Broccoli 🥦 squash, zucchini, Alkaline water 🫙Packaged Navy Beans, Lemon 🍋Bundt Cakes, zucchini bread, packaged fresh zucchini spaghetti, packaged fresh squash, Black Soap, Shea Butter, Miswak toothpaste.... Come see us!

White folk taking over what was supposed to be a black paradigm shift is causing a case of cognitive dissonance amongst our people...causing us to refuse to believe and overstand our great Ancestor John Henrik Clark's profound assertion of "WE HAVE NO FRIENDS"... stop looking thru the rose colored glasses the media is blinding US with and look at HISTORY as it applies to our struggle...now recalibrate and BLACK (block) OUT the distractions ~ Lumumba

Attention Family: Our second edition of the Black Liberation Movement newsletter "WAKE UP" is ready! For just $10 you can subscribe for the rest of this year to receive via email our publication by commenting your email address below and CashApping $10 to $blmms .....

Educate yourselves on what the REAL BLM is doing and help us build at the same time ~ Lumumba 🤎❤️

Lumumba Speaks   ~~~ Patrick Lumumba

Mad people change there condition sad people stay in the same space ~

Black humanitarianism.... do we love our enemies more than we love ourselves... tag somebody

If we force ourselves to apply the "good cop" statistic (90%-95% supposed to be good) in the George Floyd situation...then we would have to FOOLISHLY assume that there were 3 "good cops" holding Mr. Floyd down while 1 bad cop killed him!!!...see how manipulative shit can be? We have to see the world from a truly BLACK PERSPECTIVE...stop allowing the narratives to be carried by others...cause soon your life's value and even the extent of your life will be determined by OTHERS ~ Lumumba

After all the police killings of black men people still rest their hats on the sentiment that 90-95% of Cops are GOOD. Well ok...so according to that statistic how many of the 4 police bastards who killed George Floyd was supposed to be "good"? ...I'll wait ~ Lumumba

In 2017 the Black Liberation Movement with to Atlanta to take in by storm and announce ourself to the community. We connected with a lot of the minds that has been shaping our consciousness the likes of Prof. James Small, Prof. Griff (Public Enemy), Anthony Browder, Michael Imhotep, Brotha Ankh, Jay Morrison, etc..... Special shout out to my lil brotha/God son

Dre Shipp

for making sure we got there. Check us out!

Silly Negroes: "Pat stop promoting violence"

Me: "White folk don't need me to PROMOTE violence...they just need to know that you're still promoting NON-VIOLENCE with those who are violent with you ~ Lumumba

Lumumba Speaks   ~~~   Patrick Lumumba

Black "professionals" are now saying they're looking 👀 for an alternative to Starbucks...well let my not so educated, non-professional self offer a suggestion 📱...BUILD ONE! 🔨 ~ Lumumba

Y'all can send an anonymous contribution the The Black Liberation Movement...a GRASSROOTS organization that's NOT of the "newly mad" crowd of black folk that's JUST NOW mad about racism/white supremacy...we ain't just mad bout George Floyd, hell we been mad since George Stinney Jr. .... HELP US!
*CashApp $blmms

Did white supremacy ask you for permission to SHUT YOUR WORLD DOWN?...Then why would you ask them for permission to BUILD YOUR WORLD UP?...Stop thinking we need white folks to do anything...it's called SELF DETERMINATION ~ Lumumba

Meanwhile....as my people shake in our collective boots as white cops 👮continue to exercise their bloodthirst on us...we think we're safe in our INDIVIDUAL pseudo-sanctuaries until the next killing knocks on your door 🚪
~ Lumumba

#CollectiveUnity

Lumumba Speaks ~~~ Patrick Lumumba

I REFUSE to let white supremacy determine the world my black children will live in ~ Lumumba

Lumumba Speaks ~~~ Patrick Lumumba

🪴 O Ancestors.... BLACKER than a thousand Midnights.... it is to you that we owe Respect and Honor ~ Lumumba

A MORAL CHARACTER is absolutely necessary for the liberation process of our people to take place...if we don't believe that we're worth shit and act accordingly...then the expectation of others to do so is SILLY~ Lumumba

As the Guardians and Stewards of our own children's future and humanity...we should be putting the fortifications in place to ensure the day that when the world look upon our children they INSTANTLY know that they are not to be FUCKED WITH! ...... yea I could have said it better for the "grammar police" out there...but I'M SERIOUS! Are YOU?
Question: Have you ever thought about treating white, Arab, Asian, children the way ours are treated? 😨
Question: You know why you haven't? 🤔
Answer: YOU FEAR THE CONSEQUENCES!
I got 3 children...you touch any one of them...yo ass going to the CEMETERY!
That's for Donald Trump on down to a damn crackhead
~ Lumumba

We'll know that we're getting back on our natural level of existence on the planet when we see our children making sound decisions to preserve the quality of BLACK LIFE not begging a whole other race to simply exist ~ Lumumba

During the funeral processions of George Floyd something was said that was very alarming to me. A member of the Congressional Black Caucus said and I quote:
"The only CRIME George Floyd committed was being born BLACK" .....
I'm like: What he just Say? 👀What the hell?!?
Did a ranking member of the Congressional "BLACK" Caucus just say it was a crime to be born BLACK?
See this is the type weak representative leadership that can't exist moving forward....
BLACK children heard that!!?? 🏚️

Lumumba Speaks ~~~ *Patrick Lumumba*

When the National Black consciousness of changes from Black Life Matters to Black Liberation Movement...then you will know WE'RE in control...we gotta stop begging to exist ~ Lumumba

Positive don't always mean PROGRESS...
~ Lumumba

Lumumba Speaks   ~~~   Patrick Lumumba

The goal is to be EFFECTIVE not   IMPRESSIVE   ~ Lumumba

Question: In the days since George Floyd's public execution, has all the white lead protesting and white media pandering to the Christian lead black community, and repeated shooting of "dopamine" into the veins of what supposed to be an ENRAGED NO NONSENSE Black people gotten to YOU yet ~ Lumumba

Lumumba Speaks ~~~ Patrick Lumumba

Ok... I NEVER do this but the Athlete in me is still there and I been curious about something...I want to know to the people who know local football history is my brother,

Levell Alexander

, in the top 5 of running backs in Senatobia Warrior football 🏈 history?

A yes or no answer will do but if you can validate what you say... do so!

Aite wassup?!?!

On the issue of the looting that has taking place...we should understand something critical. CHAOS breds CHAOS!
Isn't it chaotic, out of order, lawless, and terrorist to murder publicly in cold blood?
Then the lawlessness, disorder, and looting "opportunist" are ONLY a result of the FIRST CHAOS!
It's Simple: Stop 🛑the first CHAOS (murder) and you don't have the second (looting) ✊~ Lumumba

Lumumba Speaks ~~~ Patrick Lumumba

White folk love to hear us BEG them for justice...STOP THIS!!! Let's move like we got a damn backbone and some MORAL CHARACTER! Stop begging and start BUILDING ~ Lumumba

Lumumba Speaks ~~~ Patrick Lumumba

I stopped talking to scared to death NEGROES who capitulate on every level possible to the systematic domination and control of white supremacy...my interest is YOUNG BLACK men and women who have MORAL CHARACTER and are not afraid to STAND UP for their own HUMANITY ~ Lumumba

#BYLC (Black Youth Leadership Coalition)

#BlackLiberationMovement

Lumumba Speaks ~~~ Patrick Lumumba

The next one of y'all that try to compare a STATE SANCTIONED MURDER by a tax paid racist to Lil Ray Ray shooting Lil Malik over a bag of skittles, a piece of crack, etc etc....I'm deleting yo ASS...and I'm not finna try to explain this shit no more...if you don't understand the gross disparities and ramifications of this by now than there's ABSOLUTELY no reason for me to waste another breath with you ~ Lumumba

#BlackLiberationMovement

Support the Agriculture Initiative of the Black Liberation Movement in these times of decision. We've not only grown your food but we've ALMOST cooked it for you! This is the first Black-To-Health box we have available for you freshly prepared to be picked up or delivered the SAME DAY! For just a $25 blessing you get:
- Freshly spiraled Zucchini spaghetti
- 2lbs of freshly cut Squash
- 2lbs of Nutritious Navy Beans
- 2 gallons of Pure Alkaline Water
- 2 packs of your choice of herbs from

Oregano, Mint, Thyme, or Basil 🌿
*Not on this list but we have a limited availability of collard greens 🥬 that can be included.
Comment below or inbox Me for ordering..(CashApp $blmms upon confirmation of order
or pay upon pickup 📦 or delivery 🚚)
REMEMBER TO SUPPORT OUR BLACK FARMERS 👨🏾‍🌾

Lumumba Speaks ~~~ Patrick Lumumba

Have WHITE PEOPLE hijacked the protests for the SOCIAL EXPERIENCE but not actual SOCIAL CHANGE 🧐... ~ Lumumba

Appreciate EVERY ONE of you who respect, believe in, and support the Black Liberation Movement...y'all the real MVP's ~ Lumumba

Lumumba Speaks   ~~~   Patrick Lumumba

Essentially a PROTEST is an appeal from the POWERLESS to the POWERFUL to stop exercising their POWER on you as it causes your discomfort...we gotta BUILD OUR OWN POWER ~ Lumumba
More to Come...Stay Tuned...

Had a conversation with a friend last week that was livid at how Derek Chauvin and the gang of white terrorists killed George Floyd...
She said: "He did that brother like a dog!
I responded: No dear, you see if it was a DOG, he would've GOT UP.
Lumumba

Lumumba Speaks ~~~ Patrick Lumumba

Why isn't the DEATH PENALTY considered in the matter of Derek Chauvin (the MURDER)? ... One day a REAL system of justice will exist...I'm gonna do my damnedest to SPEED THAT DAY UP. ~ Lumumba

Yesterday I was visited out on the land by Attorney

Malik El Shabazz

of Chicago, Illinois. He said he's been all over the country but he's not seen a comprehensive plan implemented like that of the Black Liberation Movement and he wants to add his lawful expertise. We getting STRONGER ~ Lumumba

Thanks to Lieutenant

LaCarlos Los Bowles

for photos and chauffeur.

It's the beginning of the end to our problems the moment we start CONTROLLING narratives instead of FOLLOWING them ~ Lumumba

The Black Liberation Movement represents an assertive and pragmatic approach to building POWER for our people in every area of activity, battle, and concern:

Economics

Education

Entertainment

Politics

Law

Labor

War

Sex

Religion

Health

•We have been actively engaged in Agricultural development for the past 3 years now. We seek to develop this program to an elaborate network of major food distribution.

•We have a Culture Center where we teach Black Self-Determination & National Development in Coldwater, Mississippi where we build progressive curricula from strong black educational programs such as the Oasis Literacy Center (

Crystal Denise

)...The Independence Day Project (Prof.

Carl Tone Jones

)...M.A.T.H. (

Edwar Hawkins

)...and we draw from a respectable amount of Master Teachers that we absorb knowledge, information, and guidance from.

•We have presently developed our own newsletter "WAKE UP" to document and propagandize our message that can be subscribed to by sending us your email address and small contribution of just $10 to $blmms for a digital years subscription.

•We are also developing the BYLC which is our proud Black Youth Leadership Coalition that will be our future leaders in all the areas that were mentioned above.

If you feel compelled to help us develop the Movement more, contribute financially to our efforts, our even become a member:

Donate to: $blmms

Lumumba Speaks ~~~ Patrick Lumumba

Contact us: www.blackliberationmovement.com

Peace...Blessings...and Power ~ Lumumba

It's interesting to me that all of a sudden America don't understand CAUSE & AFFECT...
Lemme explain some shit: Approximately 100 years ago TODAY white "civilians" (terrorist) along with government sanctioned military (terrorist) BURNED & AIRSTRIKED Tulsa, Oklahoma's Black business district historically known as BLACK WALL STREET! None of the participants (protesters against BLACK progress) were EVER charged as criminals for exciting a riot, burning down businesses, and I'm absolutely sure they LOOTED the goods that the Blacks of this prideful district had accumulated! Right?
300 Black people were KILLED and the survivors of this WHITE FOLK RAGE & JEALOUSY RIOT was NEVER repaired with reparations or much less apologized to....
Now...ask me again do I give a damn about America's city's burning.... and I'll ask yo ass do you give a damn about George Floyd's mother's HEART burning....
John Henrik Clark said "we need a history lesson"
Fannie Lou Hammer said "we sick and tired of being sick and tired"
Malcolm X said "the chickens will come home to roost"
For every action there's a reaction
For every cause there is an effect
Stop crying ... MORE TO COME ~ Lumumba

Lumumba Speaks   ~~~ Patrick Lumumba

We burned 🔥 the field before we planted 🌱... My point: Usually when something burns it's being purified for a new beginning...burn gotdamnit burn ~ Lumumba

Lumumba Speaks ~~~ Patrick Lumumba

I was once told by a dear friend after a talk I made that I was an Agitator...at first I was somewhat irritated by the comment, but on the drive home I thought... A washing machine is an agitator, it agitates dirty clothes till they come clean...so I embrace being an AGITATOR to my people ~ Lumumba

Lumumba Speaks ~~~ Patrick Lumumba

A DUMB sheep will follow a narrative to its doom...

A PSUEDO-intellectual sheep will articulate scholarly the same narrative but still follow it to its doom...

An INTELLIGENT sheep will just GO THE OTHER WAY...

Lumumba

#BlackLiberationMovement

Lumumba Speaks ~~~ Patrick Lumumba

www.ingramcontent.com/pod-product-compliance
Lightning Source LLC
Chambersburg PA
CBHW071158090426
42736CB00012B/2368